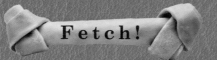

POODLES

Valerie Bodden

Creative Education

published by Creative Education
P.O. Box 227, Mankato, Minnesota 56002
Creative Education is an imprint of
The Creative Company
www.thecreativecompany.us

design and production by
Christine Vanderbeek
art direction by Rita Marshall
printed in the United States of America

photographs by Alamy (AF archive, Animal
Photography, National Geographic Image
Collection), Corbis (Bureau L.A. Collection/
Sygma), Dreamstime (Vitalij Geraskin, Issel-
ee, Lana Langlois), iStockphoto (a-wrangler,
Loretta Hostettler, rusm), Shutterstock (Eric
Isselee, Jagodka, Erik Lam, Lee319, Krissi
Lundgren, Neveshkin Nikolay, PCHT, Ti
Santi, Viorel Sima, Toloubaev Stanislav,
Nikolai Tsvetkov, WilleeCole)

library of congress
cataloging-in-publication data
Bodden, Valerie.
Poodles / Valerie Bodden.
p. cm. — (Fetch!)
SUMMARY: A brief overview of the physical
characteristics, personality traits, and habits
of the poodle breed, as well as descrip-
tions of famous pop-culture poodles such
as Georgette.
Includes index.

ISBN 978-1-60818-363-0
1. Poodles—Juvenile literature. I. Title.
SF429.P85B594 2014
636.72'8—dc23   2013005519

first edition
9 8 7 6 5 4 3 2 1

TABLE OF CONTENTS

PLAYFUL POODLES

A poodle is a *breed* of dog. Poodles are smart, playful dogs. They like to please their owners by following commands.

WHAT DO POODLES LOOK LIKE?

There are three kinds of poodles. Toy poodles are only 10 inches (25 cm) tall. They weigh about as much as a newborn human baby. Miniature poodles are about as tall as a ruler. They weigh between 12 and 18 pounds (5–8 kg). Standard poodles can be more than 20 inches (51 cm) tall and weigh up to 65 pounds (29 kg).

Toy, miniature, and standard poodles are pictured above (left to right).

All poodles have oval-shaped heads with a long *muzzle*. They have dark eyes and long, fluffy ears. Their tails are *docked*. Poodles have curly fur covering most of their bodies. Their fur can be black, white, brown, gray, or red.

POODLE PUPPIES

Newborn poodle puppies weigh less than one pound (0.5 kg). A puppy born with black fur might grow up to have gray fur. A puppy born with dark brown fur might later have light brown fur.

A poodle puppy sometimes has wavy fur that gets curlier later on.

POODLES ON-SCREEN

Poodles can be seen in many movies and cartoons. Cleo is a poodle on the TV show *Clifford the Big Red Dog*. In the movie *Babe: Pig in the City*, a pig named Babe rescues a stray poodle that has been **dyed** pink.

Babe helps his dog friends in the movie (left).

POODLES AND PEOPLE

Hundreds of years ago, poodles were first used as hunting dogs. Some pulled carts or herded sheep. In the 1700s, poodles became performers in circuses. Today, many poodles work as **therapy dogs**.

Poodles jumped through hoops and did tricks in the circus (right).

Poodles are very good with kids. But toy poodles may be too small for very young children. Toy and miniature poodles can be good pets for people who live in apartments. Standard poodles usually need more space. Both male and female poodles make good pets.

Tiny poodles make good city dogs.

WHAT DO POODLES LIKE TO DO?

Standard poodles need a lot of exercise. Miniature and toy poodles need some exercise every day, too. Poodles should be brushed every day. They need to have their fur clipped often.

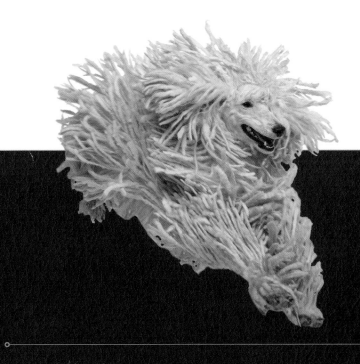

Poodles do not shed, so they need their fur to be cut regularly.

Fetch!

Poodles love to spend time with their owners. And they love to swim. Take your poodle to a pond and jump in. You will both have lots of fun!

A FAMOUS POODLE

Georgette is a standard poodle in the Walt Disney movie *Oliver & Company*. She is a **show dog** owned by a rich family. Georgette is selfish and likes to get her way. At first, she does not want to share her home with a stray kitten named Oliver. But by the end of the movie, Georgette has become kinder to Oliver.

GLOSSARY

breed a kind of an animal with certain traits, such as long ears or a good nose

docked made shorter by cutting off the end

dyed changed to a different color

muzzle an animal's nose and mouth

show dog a dog that competes in dog shows, where judges decide which dogs are the best examples of each breed

therapy dogs dogs that help people who are sick or hurt by letting the people pet and enjoy them

READ MORE

Fitzpatrick, Anne. *Poodles*. North Mankato, Minn.: Smart Apple Media, 2004.

Johnson, Jinny. *Poodle*. North Mankato, Minn.: Smart Apple Media, 2013.

Schuh, Mari C. *Poodles*. Minneapolis: Bellwether Media, 2009.

WEBSITES

Bailey's Responsible Dog Owner's Coloring Book
http://classic.akc.org/pdfs/public_education/coloring_book.pdf
Print out pictures to color, and learn more about caring for a pet dog.

Just Dog Breeds: Standard Poodle
http://www.justdogbreeds.com/poodle.html
Learn more about standard poodles, and check out lots of poodle pictures.